本书惠承乐俊民严赛虹基金会赞助出版

The publication of this anthology is sponsored by

Iris and Junming Le Foundation

诗句口香糖

（有味道就多嚼嚼，没有就吐掉）

Chewing Gum Verses

(Chew on them if they taste good, otherwise spit them out)

2015—2025

严力 Yan Li

Translated by Glen Aaron Steinman (斯仲達)

Edited by Professor Ruan Danqing (阮丹青教授)

易文出版社

I Wing Press, New York

Chewing Gum Verses *(Chew on them if they taste good, otherwise spit them out)* 2015-2025

By Yan Li

Artwork: Yan Li
Publisher: Paul Qiu
Book Design: Wang Changhua

Published by I Wing Press, New York
iwingpress@gmail.com
May 2026, First Edition, First Printing
ISBN: 978-1-961768-32-1 (Paperback)
           979-8-3493-3745-1 (eBook)

诗句口香糖（有味道就多嚼嚼，没有就吐掉）2015-2025

严力 著

艺术作品：严　力
装帧设计：王昌华
出 版 人：邱辛晔

出　版：　易文出版社·纽约
版　次：　2026 年 5 月 第 1 版，第 1 次印刷
定　价：　$30.00

1

别说了，动刀叉吧

既然在餐桌的席位上

就不在菜单上

Stop talking, just use your knife and fork

Since you have a seat at the dining table

You are not on the menu

2

我信仰诗神、酒神、善良的眼神

I believe in the god of poetry, the god of wine and divine
kind eyes

3

政客们形容着

枕头里的各种想法

常常忘了还没有床

Politicians describe

All sorts of thoughts inside their pillows

Often forgetting they still don't have a bed

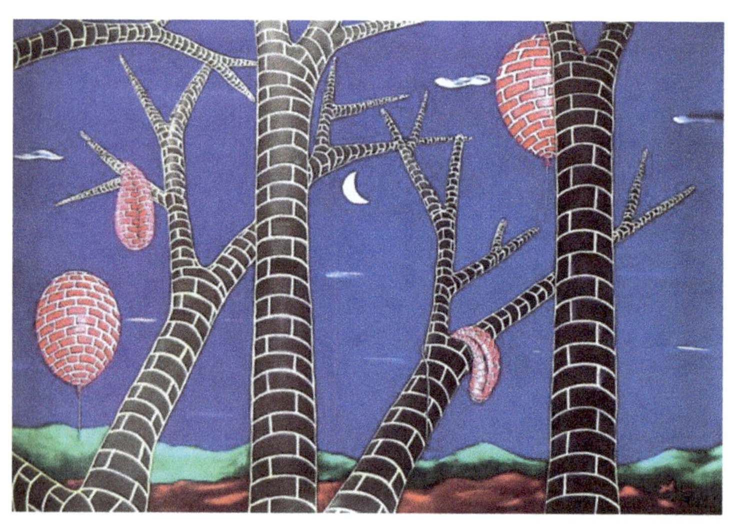

那里是家园 / There Is Home

丙烯画 / Acrylic Painting。135X175 CM. 2004.

4

除了人类

动植物都有坚定的地球立场

Other than humans

Animals and plants stand firmly on the earth

5

本能只能进化成本能

Instinct can only evolve into instinct

6

旁观者必须是单身

The onlooker must be single

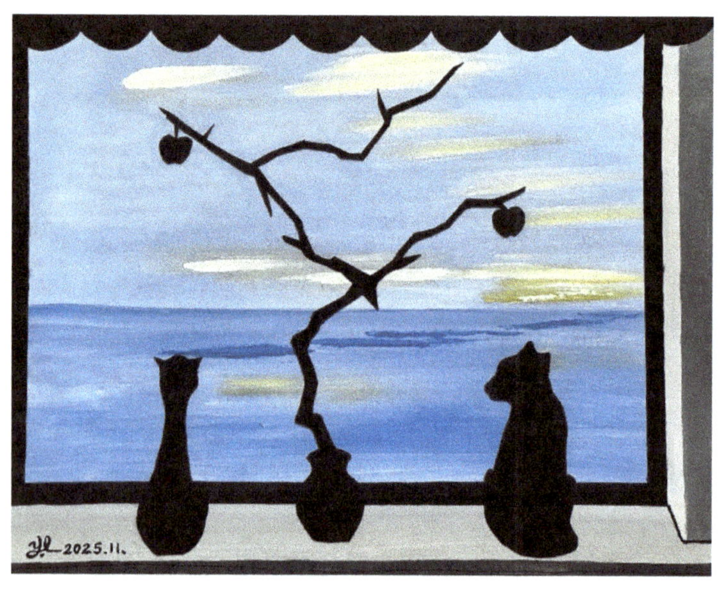

还在等待苹果跌落的时刻/Still Waiting for the Moment the Apple Falls

丙烯画 / Acrylic Painting。 135X175 CM. 2004.

7

有了贫富差距之后

物理差异还重要吗

Once there is a gap between rich and poor

Do physical disparities still matter

8

无论是社会还是年龄造成的

词语试图拉直弯下去的脊椎

Whether bent spines are caused by society or age

Words try to straighten them

9

良知是人间唯一的故乡

可以随身携带

Conscience is the world's only homeland

It can be carried everywhere

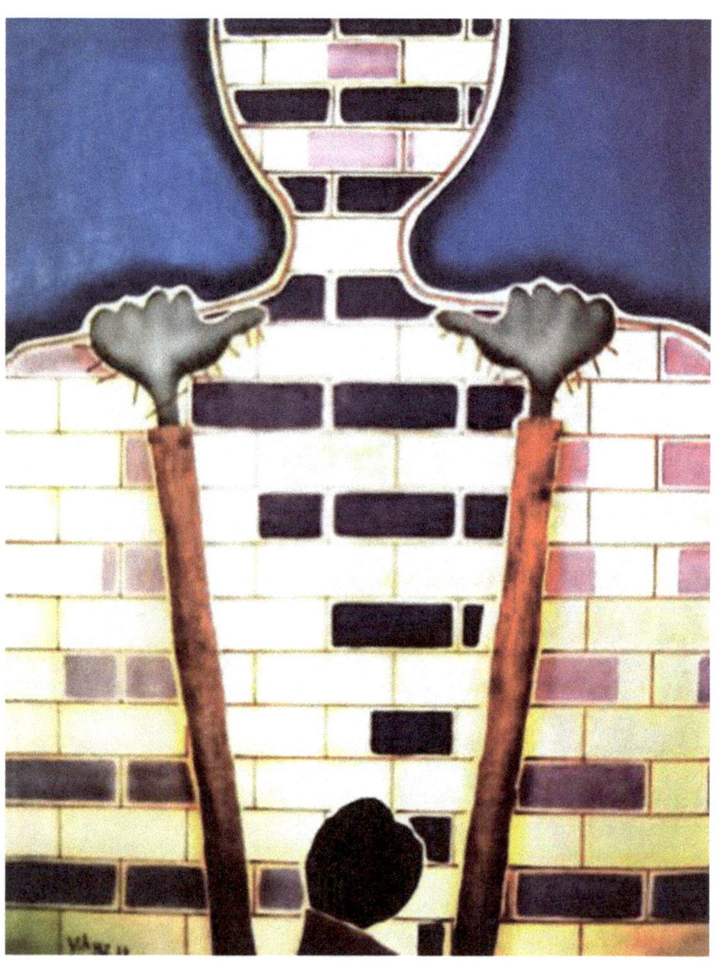

被缝在都市里的人 / People Sewn into the City

丙烯画 / Acrylic Painting。 135X175 CM. 2004.

真假信息都是人生产出来的

Real and fake news are both manufactured by people

11

怀旧者继续在暗房里洗印上世纪的青春

而当代人在点击键盘时直接失去了青春

Nostalgists stay in the darkroom developing images of their youth in the last century

Modern people lose youth when clicking their keyboards

12

"反省"是生产精神食粮的大省

"Self-reflection" is a large province that produces spiritual nourishment

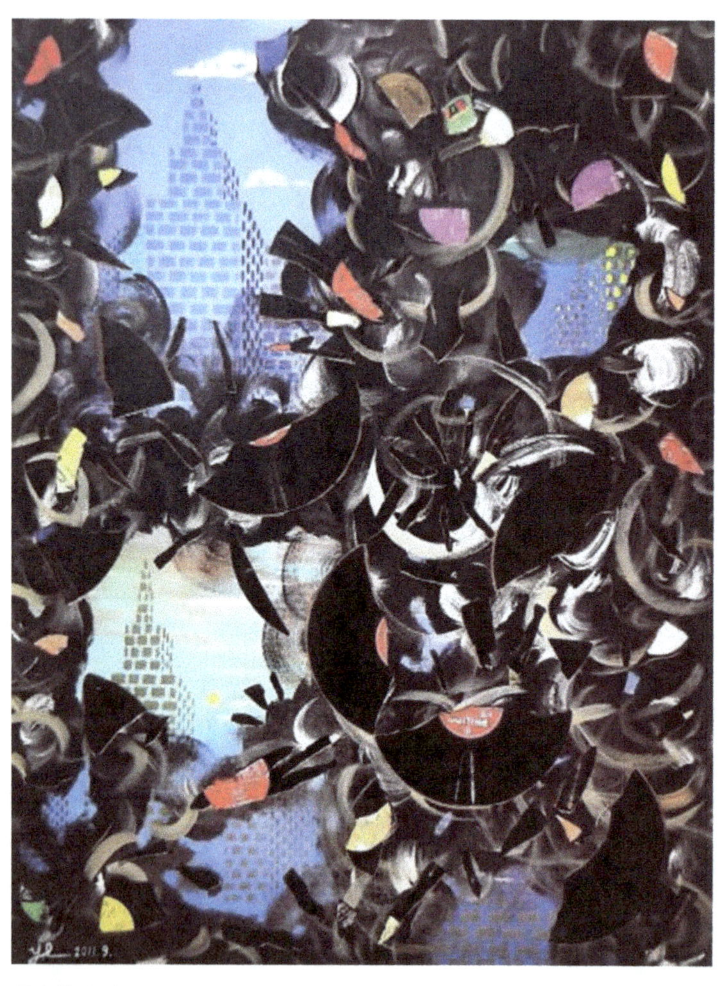

都市综合症 / Urban Syndrome

丙烯画、黑胶唱片画 / Acrylic Painting, Vinyl Record Painting。

135X175 CM. 2011.

大熊猫存世上千年了

但它被搬上画面的历史只有五十几年

其原因是源于竹子

它因嫉妒和仇恨没把熊猫介绍给人类

Giant pandas have existed for thousands of years

Yet the history of painting them on rice paper is only fifty years old

This is because of bamboo

It did not introduce pandas to humans out of jealousy and resentment

14

仅仅用风、水与时间作为创作工具

大自然写出了石头上所有的诗

Using only wind, water and time as creative tools

Nature wrote all its poetry on stones

15

无语和沉默是人类常用的母语

Speechlessness and silence are the common native
language of humans

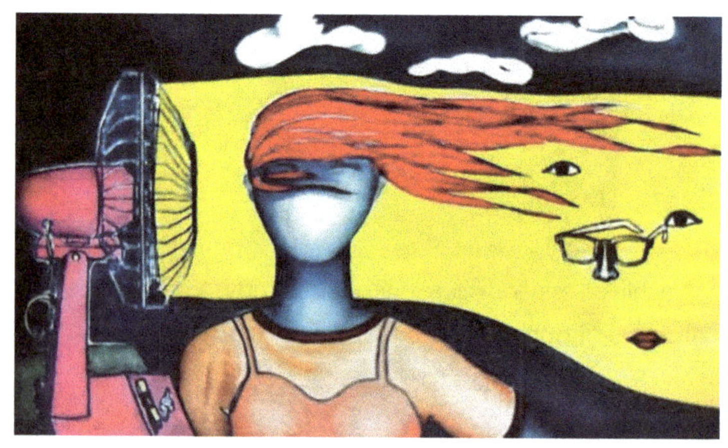

电风扇的隐形功能 / The Invisible Function of an Electric Fan

丙烯画 / Acrylic Painting。 55X110 CM. 1980.

_16_

其他动物听不懂什么不是动物，什么不是人

Other animals don't comprehend what isn't an animal and
what isn't a human

17

"良人"很难准确地翻译成英文

甚至从中文翻译到中文也很难

The term "Liang Ren" is difficult to translate to English

Even translating it from Chinese to Chinese is difficult

("Liang Ren" connotes both a "good person" and carries additional layers of meanings)

18

我和鱼缸里的热带鱼的共同点

就是都需要舒服的温度

My similarity with tropical fish in a tank

Is we both need a comfortable temperature

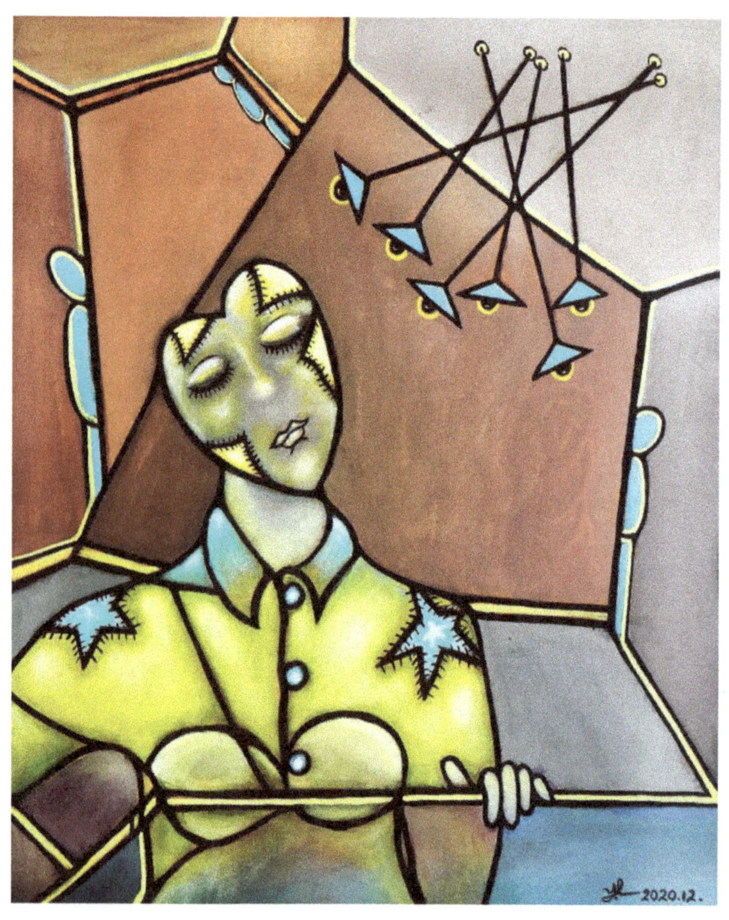

寂寞的时刻有各自的故事 / Lonely Moments Have Their Own Stories
丙烯画 / Acrylic Painting。 60X76 CM. 2020.

19

作为个人我寻找人类

作为人类我寻找个人

As an individual I seek humanity

As part of humanity I seek the individual

20

想不通的是：

把"我"翻译成"自己"时

为何从一个字变成了两个字

I can't figure this out:

When translating "I" as "one's self"

Why does one word become two

(The Chinese character "我" means "I," while the two-character term "自己" means self and can also be understood as "one's self.")

21

一百米冲刺也是文明的极限

你怎么跑也进不了九秒以内

A hundred-metre sprint is the outer edge of civilization

You can't break nine seconds no matter how you run

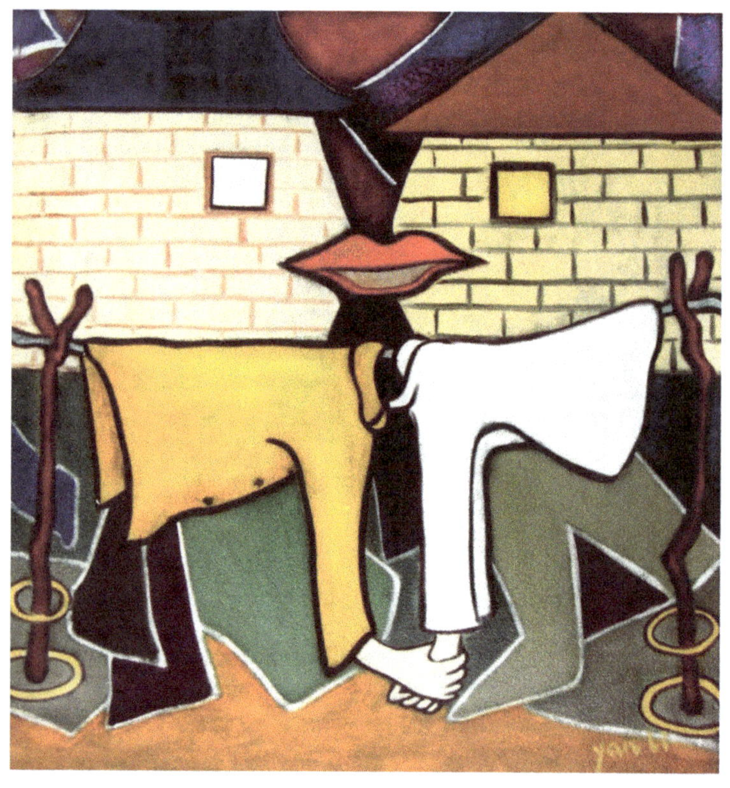

邻里关系 / Neighborhood Relations

油画 / Oil Painting。 70X72 CM. 1980.

22

把太阳从地平线下提前挖出来后

发现明天还没成为历史

只能把它再埋下去

After prematurely digging up the sun from below the horizon

We find that tomorrow has not yet become history

So we must rebury it

23

每次被梦想叮醒

都发现没地方挠

Each time a dream stings me awake

I find nowhere to scratch

24

在使用语言之前

先熟悉一下牙缝

Before using language

First get to know the gaps between your teeth

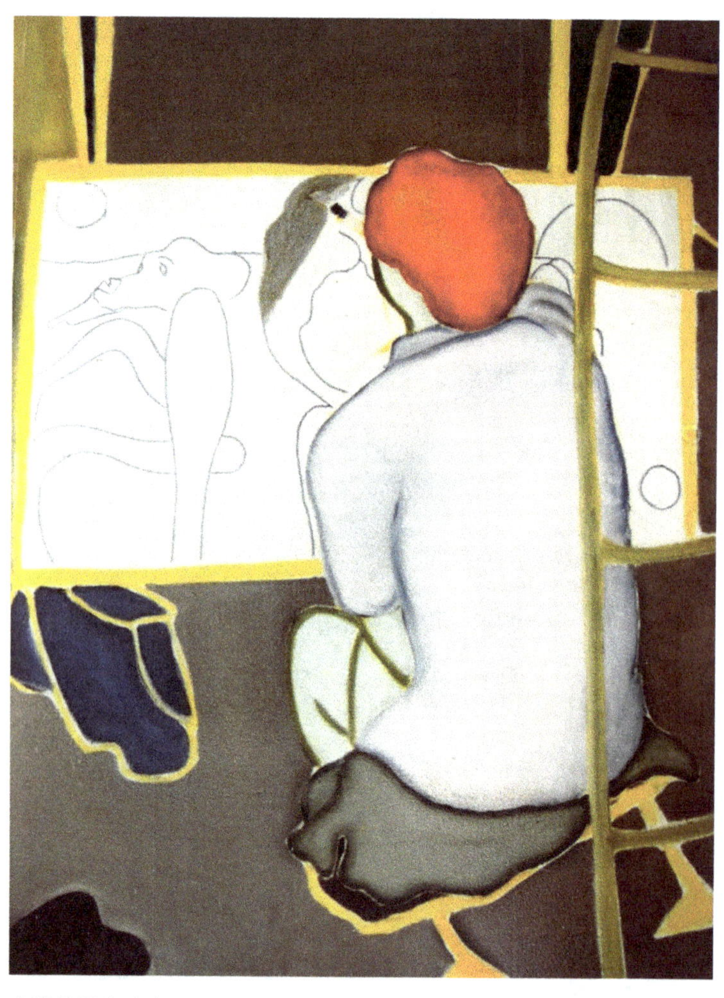

安静的画家 / The Quiet Painter

油画 / Oil Painting。 68X76 CM. 1979.

25

最原始的理想就是

把病床和手术台从人类身上切除

In the most primal ideal

The sickbed and operating table are cut out of the human body

26

再出席千万次地球上的葬礼

诗歌手中的悼词还是用不完

After attending countless funerals on earth

Poetry's hands still hold an endless store of elegies

如果你能保持独立思考的习惯

汗水也就能舔着自己的盐生存

If you can maintain the habit of thinking independently

Sweat can survive by licking its own salt

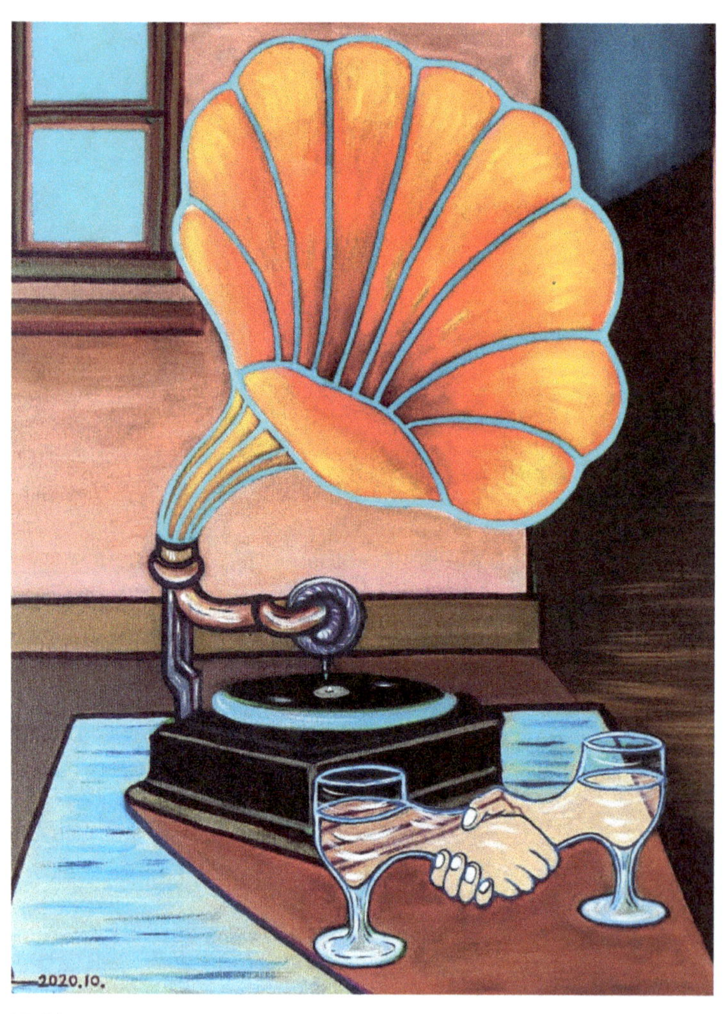

酒逢知己 / Wine Meets a Kindred Spirit

丙烯画 / Acrylic Painting。 60X76 CM. 2020.

28

白纸无限厚

挖掘无止境

Blank paper has no limit to its depth

Excavation never ends

29

拧开心中的瓶盖喝酒吧

醉就醉在自己的度数中

Twist open your heart's bottle cap and drink the wine inside

If you get drunk enjoy it at your own "proof"

30

脚踏两只船时

紧张的是睾丸

When stepping into two boats at once

It's the testicles that get tense

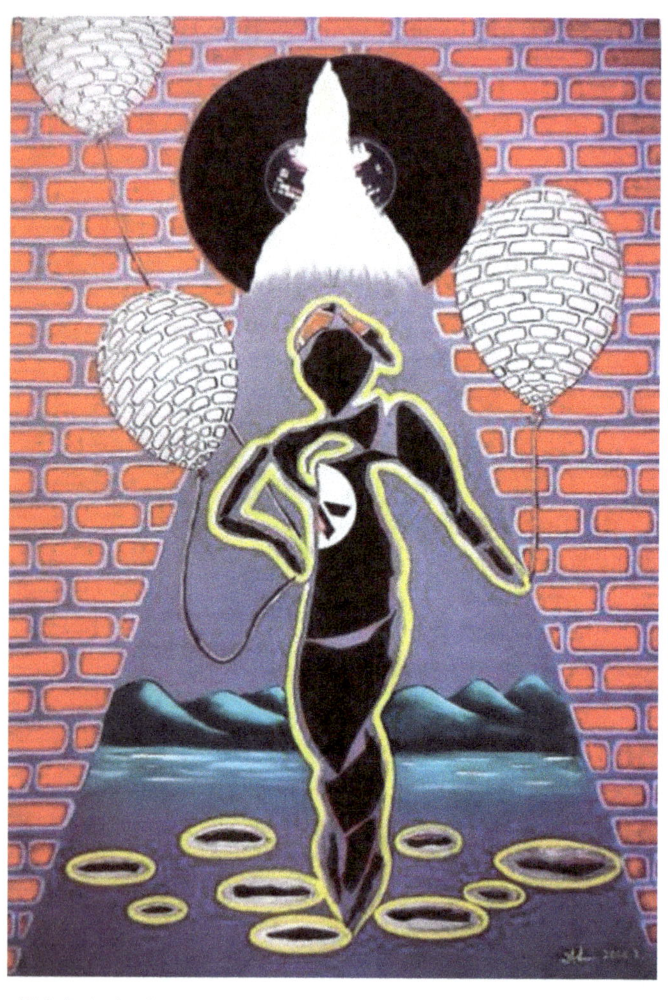

都市舞台 / Urban Stage

丙烯画、黑胶唱片画 / Acrylic Painting, Vinyl Record Painting。

76X100 CM. 2006.

31

我保持着带几首诗上路的习惯

它比带几箱饼干更能找到知己

I have the habit of taking a few poems on the road

They are better than boxes of cookies at finding kindred souls

32

信仰与利益的关系

无非是舅舅和外甥

或者是姑姑与侄女

Faith's relationship with self-interest

Is like that of an uncle and his sister's son

Or an aunt and her brother's daughter

33

不涉及两边的景色

火车过去后

背影在两条铁轨上

It is not about the scenery on each side

After the train passes by

The rear image remains on the two train tracks

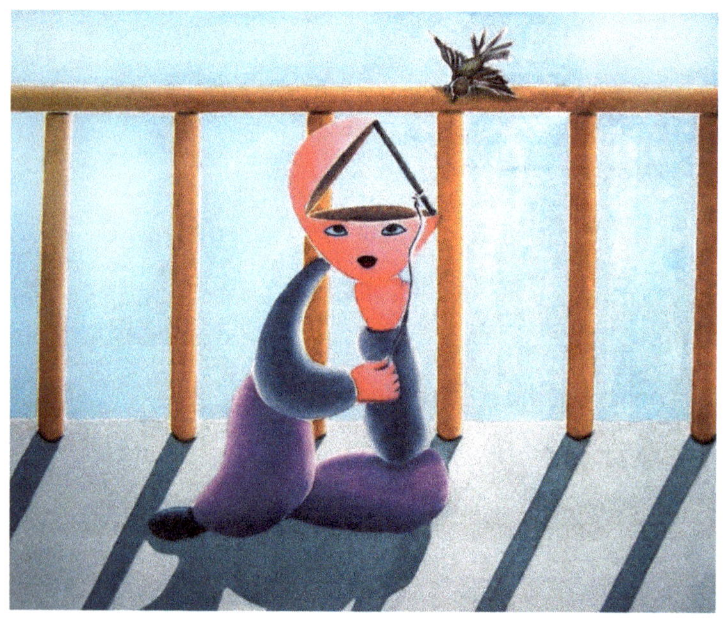

捕捉自由 / Capturing Freedom

油画 / Oil Painting。 70X72 CM. 1982.

34

高调的感恩

不是语言的本意

Grandiose gratitude

Is not language's original intent

35

眼睛的观点是：

颜色比事实可靠

From the eye's perspective

Color is more reliable than fact

没什么计划

只是跟着社会地势的森林走

沿下坡路打猎的老人中

有一位号称我

Having no plan

I merely move through the forest of the social terrain

Those elders hunting downhill

Include one called "I"

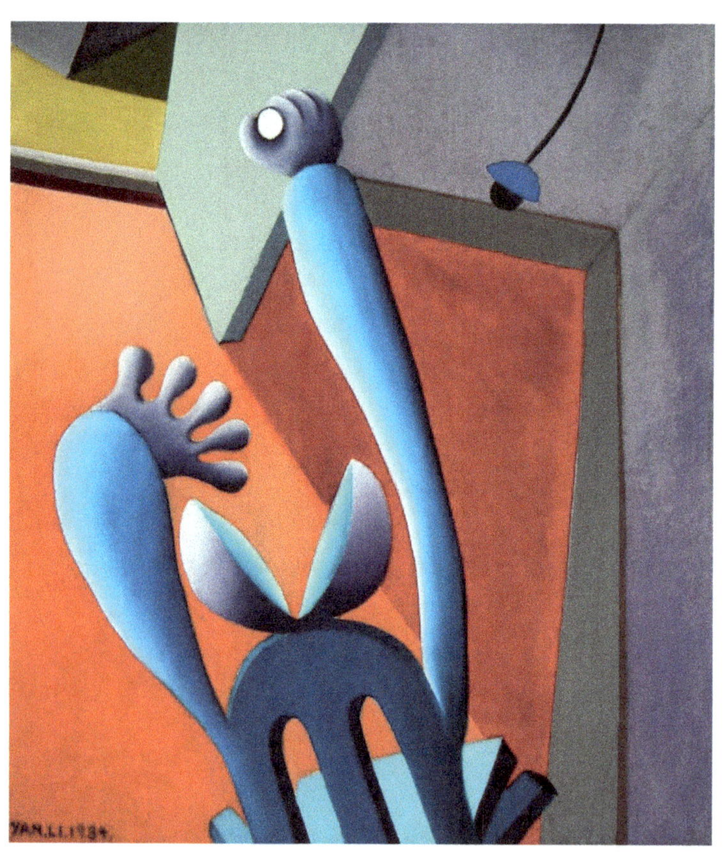

连椅子都想离家出走 / *Even the Chair Wants to Leave Home*

油画 / *Oil Painting*。 76X100 CM. 1984.

陪我爸喝闷酒的理由很简单

他饱受理想的压迫

但他依然以压不弯的口气说

你随意我干了

The reason for drinking alone with my father in silence is simple

He suffered the full weight of ideals

Yet with a voice that still won't bow to pressure he says

Drink yours as you wish while I gulp mine down

38

无聊时就与枕套的花纹聊聊你的发型

When bored just chat with the pillowcase pattern about
your hairstyle

与输赢无关

只有挖出与身体同等体积的泥土

才能躺进死亡

It's not about winning or losing

Only by digging a volume of earth equal to that of the
body

Can one lie into death

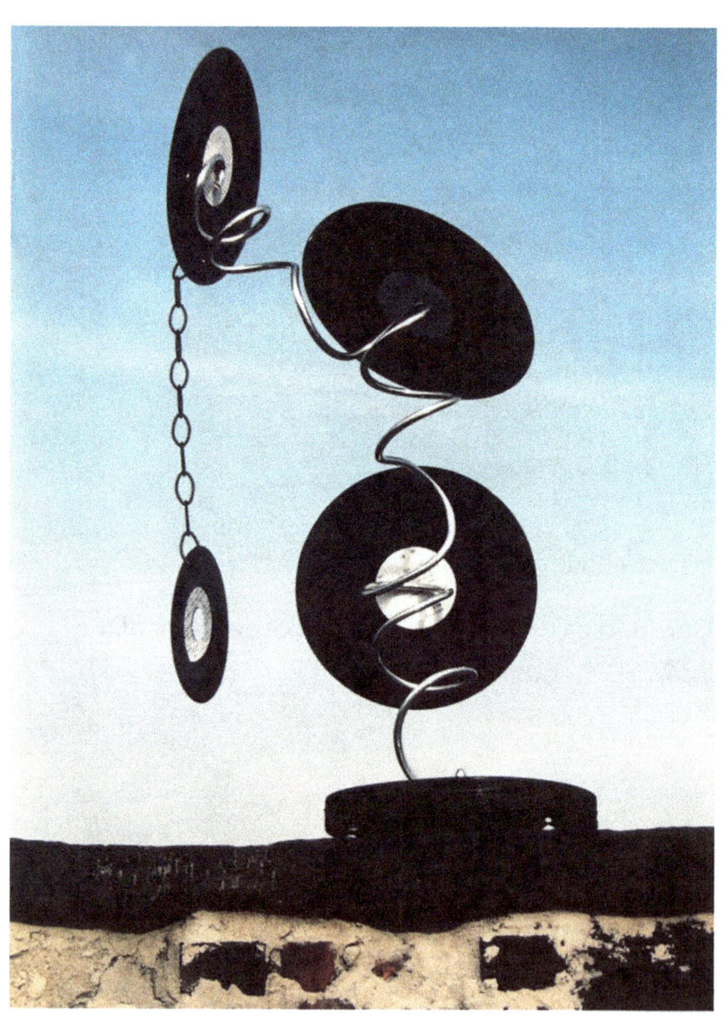

固定的音乐 / Fixed Music

唱片雕塑 / Record Sculpture。 55X100 CM. 1988.

40

坏就坏在你更享受坏人对你的赞美

What's truly bad is that you take even greater pleasure
when bad people praise you

41

很多人都是心里有话却没人进来的酒吧

Many people are taverns with bottled-up words and no
one entering to listen

土地没有庄稼意识

我们收工

土地不收

The land is not conscious of crops

When we finish our work

The land does not

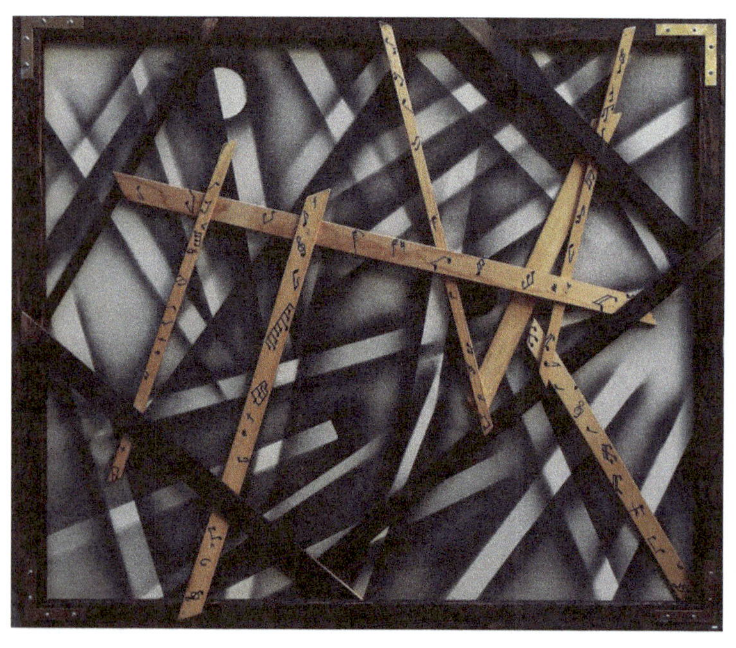

穿梭在都市里的光 / Light Shuttling Through the City

喷漆、木条等 / Spray Paint, Wood Strips, etc.。76X100 CM. 1987.

43

叹号的生活形象更新了

扶着扫帚的人都通着电

The living form of an exclamation point has been updated

Now it is a person holding a broom upright with electricity flowing through him

44

如今三句话里有两句都戴着口罩

These days two of every three sentences wear a mask

45

过期护照都住在以前的国家里

All expired passports live in their former countries

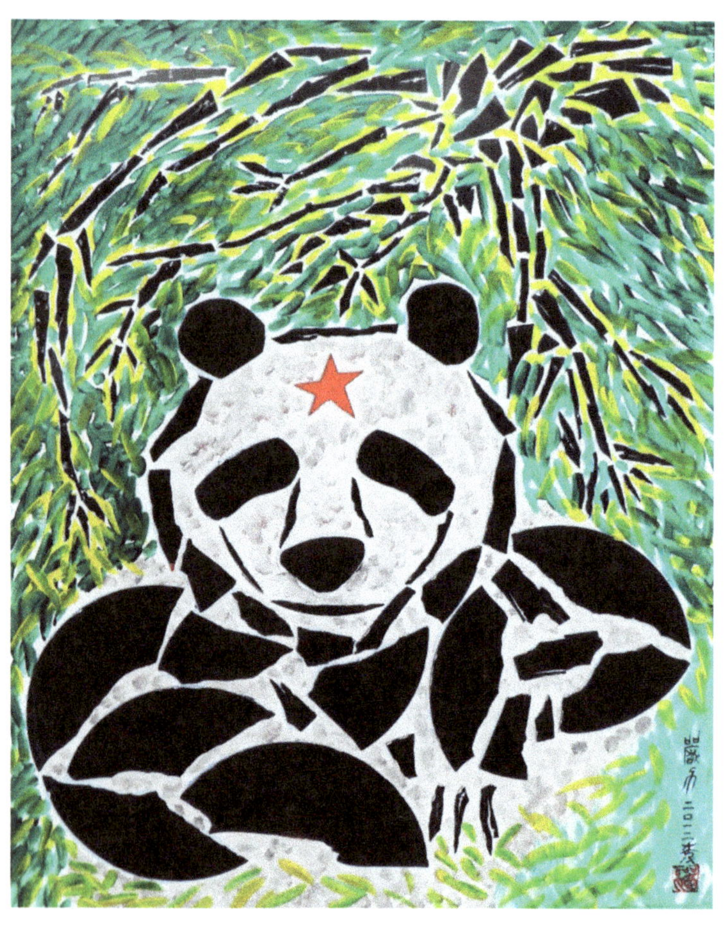

熊猫大使 / Panda Ambassador

丙烯、黑胶唱片画 / Acrylic, Vinyl Record Painting。 76X100 CM. 2012.

有神论者相信历史奇迹

反之则呼唤今天的皇帝

People who believe in God also believe in historical miracles

Others seek an Emperor today

走上历史遗留下来的道路后

我的鞋里全都是以前的脚印

After walking paths history left behind

My shoes are filled with footprints from the past

48

人生需要避免的是

为两只并排的鸟而喜欢那棵树

Life requires avoiding

Loving a tree because two birds are perched side by side
on it

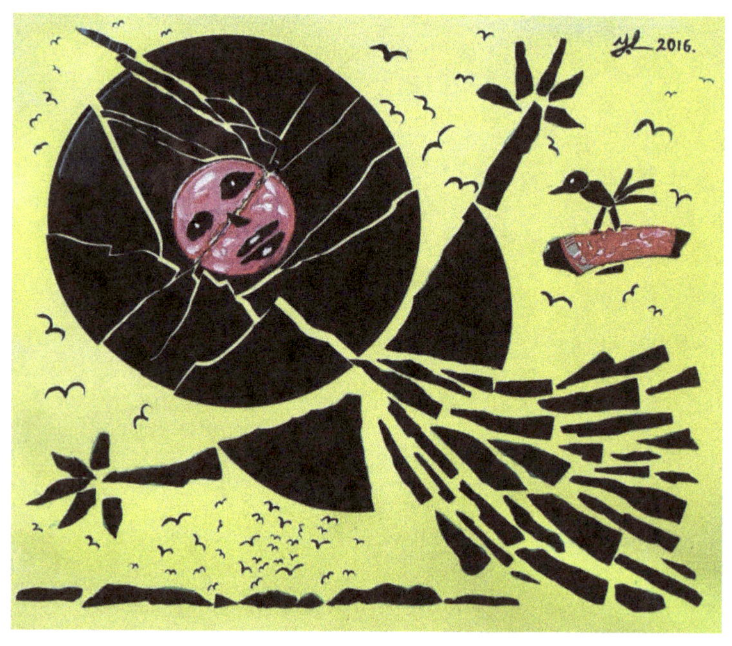

万圣节 / Halloween

丙烯、黑胶唱片画 / Acrylic, Vinyl Record Painting。 55X66 CM. 2016.

49

坚持的意义在于

没有人能坚持到

悬挂想法的枝杈

不再发芽

Persistence means

No one can persist until

Branches where ideas hang

Stop sprouting

50

洗脑后形成的愚蠢基于那张白纸

Stupidity born of brainwashing is based on a blank sheet of paper

51

宁静是内心居住的永久空间

不需要按时代的变化而搬家

Serenity is the mind's eternal dwelling space

It need not relocate with the changing times

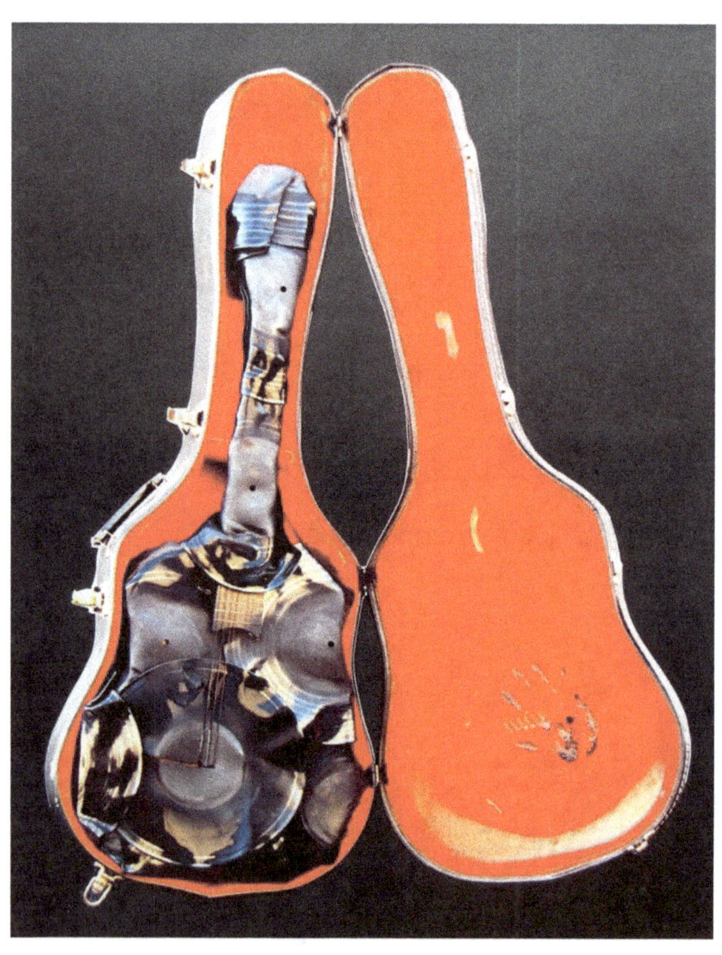

吉他的葬礼 / The Guitar's Funeral

雕塑：吉他、黑胶唱片、盒子 / Sculpture: Guitar, Vinyl Record, Box。
76X120 CM. 1987.

52

有人喜欢春天

有人喜欢变天

Some people love spring

Some people love upheaval

53

风不知道旗帜把它拦进了信仰的方向

The wind does not know a flag has boxed it into an
ideological path

54

一旦劳动的方向错了

就不如不劳动

为此我很自豪地

做过多年不劳动的人民

Once the direction of work is wrong

It's better not to work at all

For this I have proudly

Been among those who have not worked for many years

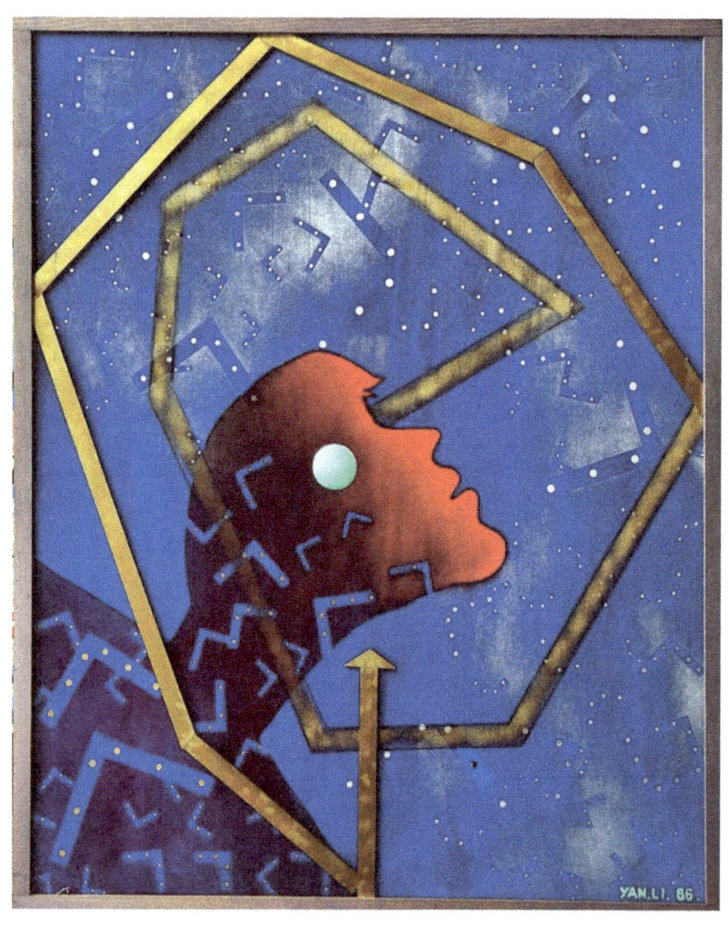

展望互联网 / Looking Toward the Internet

喷漆、丙烯、木条等 / Spray Paint, Acrylic, Wood Strips, etc.。

135X175 CM. 1986.

55

简单的生活并不意味着

你就远离了复杂的人性

A simple life does not mean

You are far from human nature's complexity

56

眺望的姿势是我多年看到的风景

The posture of gazing into the distance is the view I have
seen for many years

57

世界一直有戏

但不证明它越演越好

而是可以去倒卖戏票

The world has always been theater

But this does not mean the performance keeps improving

It is only that you can scalp the ticket to the show

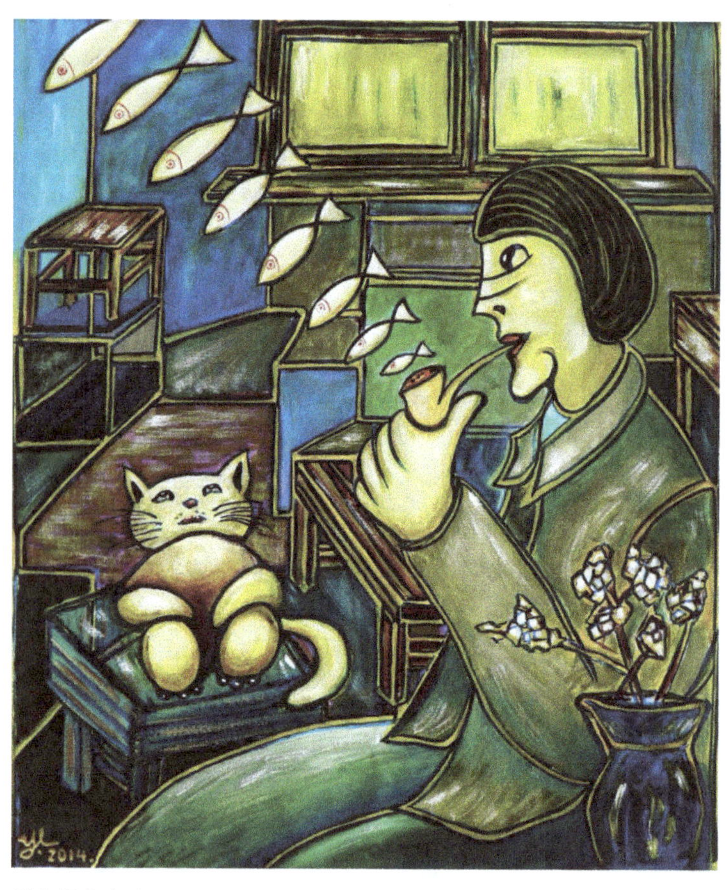

猫的想象力 / A Cat's Imagination

丙烯画 / Acrylic Painting。 76X100 CM. 2014.

58

医生说你的身体应该拒绝甜品了

但是，可以与糖纸偷情

Doctors say you should refuse sweets for your health

But you can still have a secret love affair with a candy wrapper

59

说到时尚和潮流

我喜欢在被淘汰的沙发上

体会二手舒服

Speaking of fashion and trends

I like being on a discarded sofa

Experiencing secondhand comfort

60

倾斜的山坡

总令我感觉后腿的快感

Sloping hillsides

Always give me the pleasure of hind legs

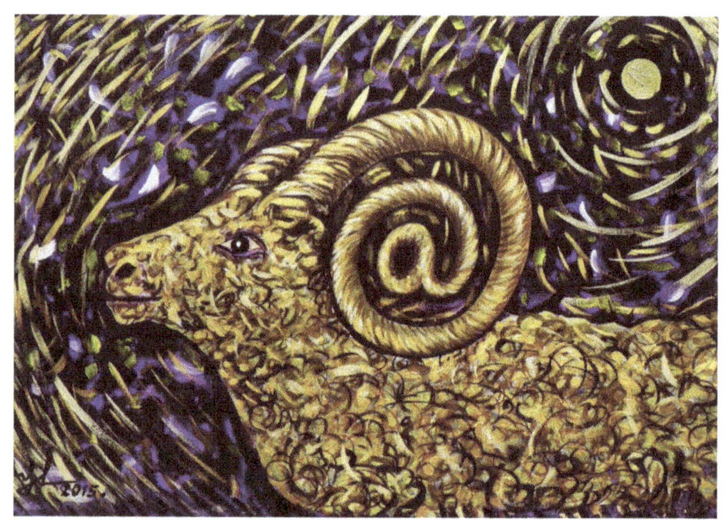

羊年的生长趋势 / Growth Trend in the Year of the Goat

丙烯画 / Acrylic Painting。 60X78 CM. 2015.

61

每当我深感悲哀时

影子都会朝向快乐

Each time I feel deep sorrow

My shadow orients toward joy

62

没有拿不动手段的手

只有拿和不拿的区分

No hands are incapable of taking measures

The only difference among them is taking them or not

63

高科技升级了生活便利

但不负责升级你的尊严

High-tech has upgraded life's convenience

But is not responsible for upgrading your dignity

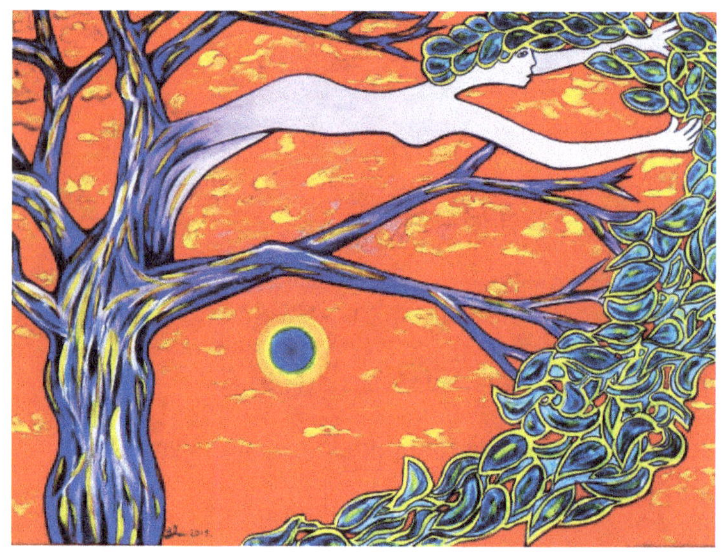

对秋意的挽留 / Holding on to Autumn

丙烯画 / Acrylic Painting。90X130 CM. 2015.

64

大家都度过了每天喝水

但影子不会出汗的一生

Everyone has spent a lifetime

Drinking water each day while their shadows never sweat

65

放纵欲望就是罪被犯罪者盯上了

Criminals target the sin of indulging desire

66

最近的消息很新奇

避孕套戴在了黄瓜身上

The recent news is very strange

A cucumber is wearing a condom

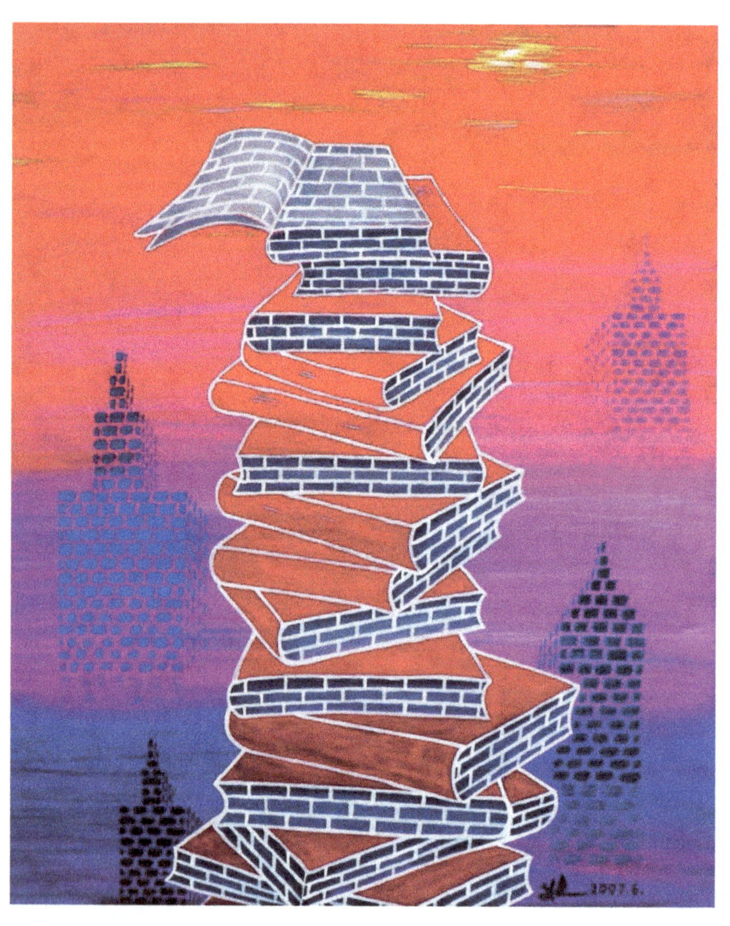

上层建筑 / Superstructure

丙烯画 / Acrylic Painting。 76X100 CM. 2007.

67

自恋就是把刀和刀鞘铸成了

不能分开的一体

Narcissism is the melding of a knife and its sheath

Into a single inseparable whole

68

有些人用一生的奔波

还是错过了很多个家

Some people spend a lifetime rushing around

Yet they miss out on many homes along the way

69

我的视线被经济衰退

打了一个又一个结

从这样的视线看出去

全是饿一顿饱一顿的风景

My vision is tied up by economic recession

One knot after another

When looking out from this perspective

All I see are alternating scenes of hunger and satedness

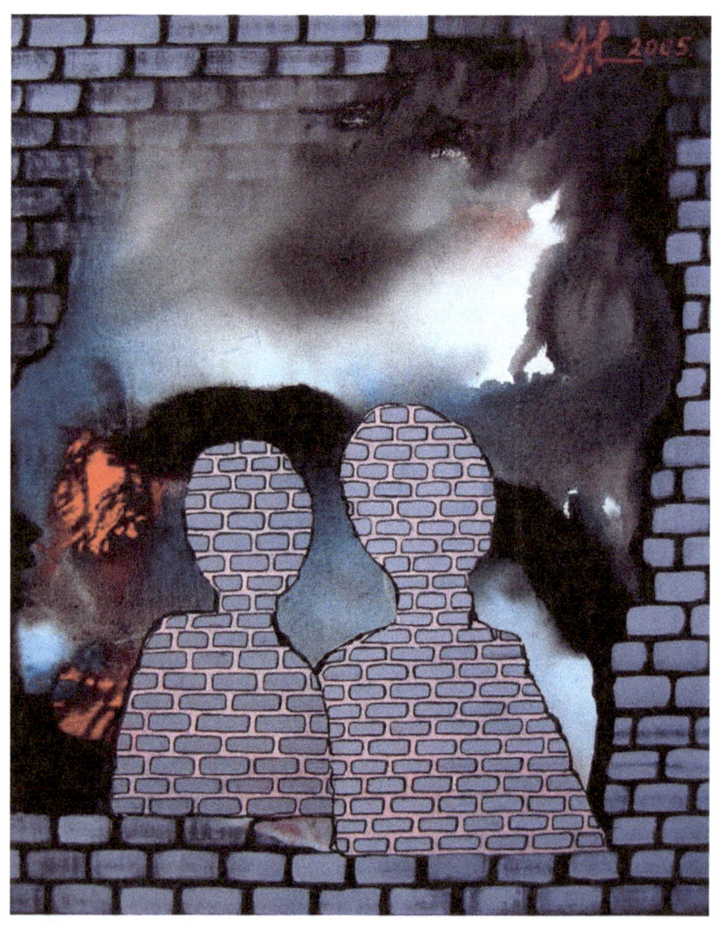

拆迁的硝烟 / Smoke of Demolition

丙烯画 / Acrylic Painting。 76X100 CM. 2005.

70

很多人抓住感叹词不放

也就分不清

手和栏杆了

Many people cling to exclamatory words

Unable to decipher

Hands from railings

71

不是所有的底部都可以卧底

但卧底肯定在底部的尺寸里

Not every underground can hold a spy

But a spy is certainly within the underground's bounds

72

春雨和美妙的滴嗒声是两件事

Spring rain and its wondrous pitter-patter are two different things

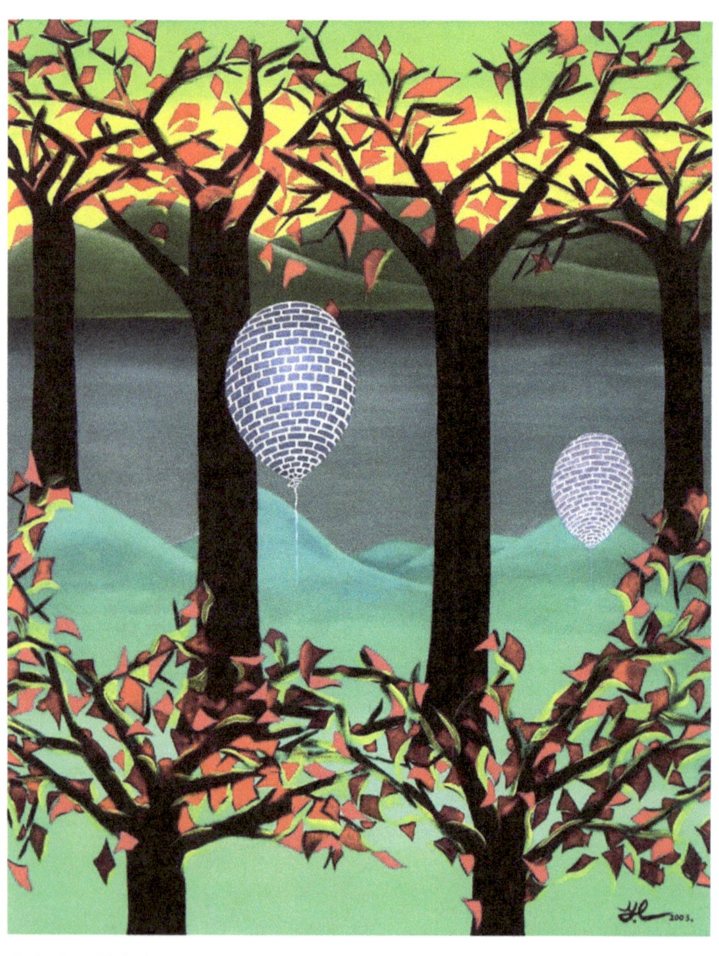

住在砖头里向往大自然的人们 / People Living in Bricks, Longing for Nature
丙烯画 / Acrylic Painting。 135X175 CM. 2003.

73

故事讲着讲着

不是桨断了就是河流断了

最后还是要交给故事处理

A story is told and told

Either the oar breaks or the river runs dry

Let the story handle it in the end

74

我想请生活吃一顿

令它此生难忘的美食

结果发现还轮不上我请客

I want to treat Life

To a gourmet meal it will not forget

But it turns out it is not yet my turn to host

人类无法用血缘关系

继承善良的行为

Humans cannot use blood ties

To inherit kind behavior

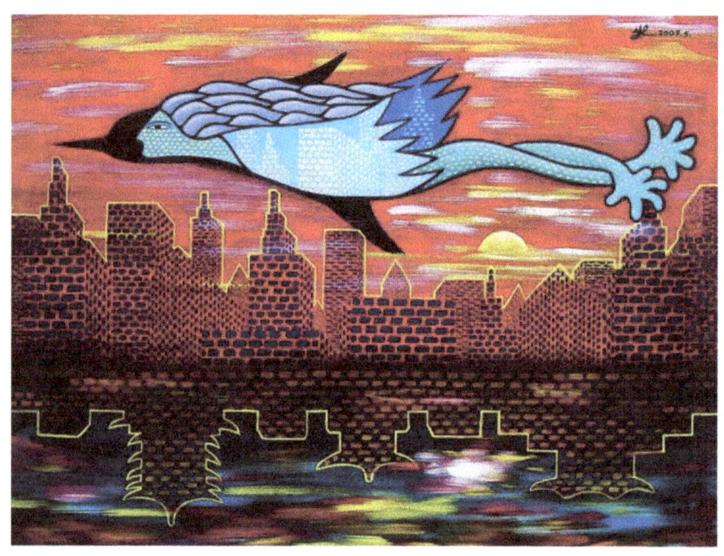

北京的灵魂 / The Soul of Beijing

丙烯画 / Acrylic Painting。90X120 CM. 2009.

76

面对不会干枯的欲望之井

所有的节省显然是徒劳的

Facing a well of desire that never runs dry

All restraint is clearly in vain

77

造物者在阅读我们手上那本拿反的书

The Creator is reading the book we are holding upside down

78

想起了小时候的逃学

就是想不起去了哪里

I remember skipping school as a kid

But I can't remember where I went

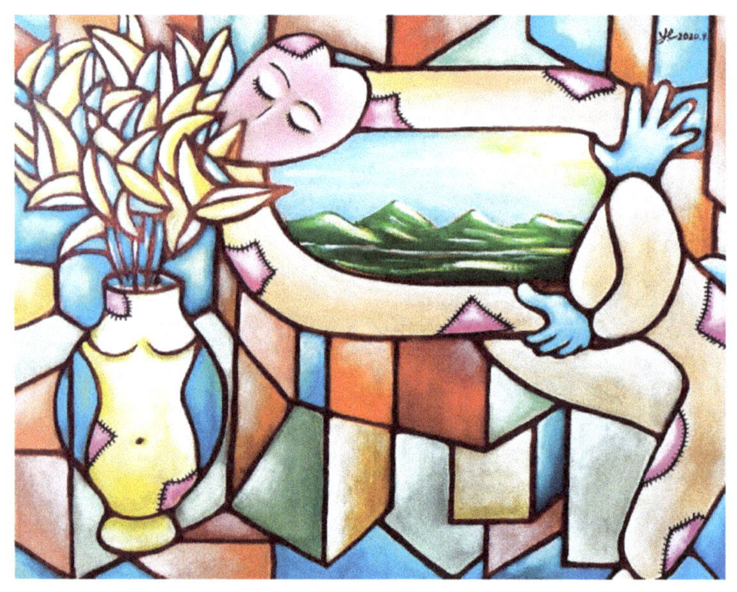

花朵的体香 / The Body Fragrance of Flowers

丙烯画 / Acrylic Painting。 60X76 CM. 2020.

79

我们生活在模仿生活的生活中

We live inside a life that imitates life

80

风俗太多也就没有了风俗

Custom ceases to exist when there are too many customs

81

我喜欢舒服的思想胜于沙发

I prefer comfortable thoughts to sofas

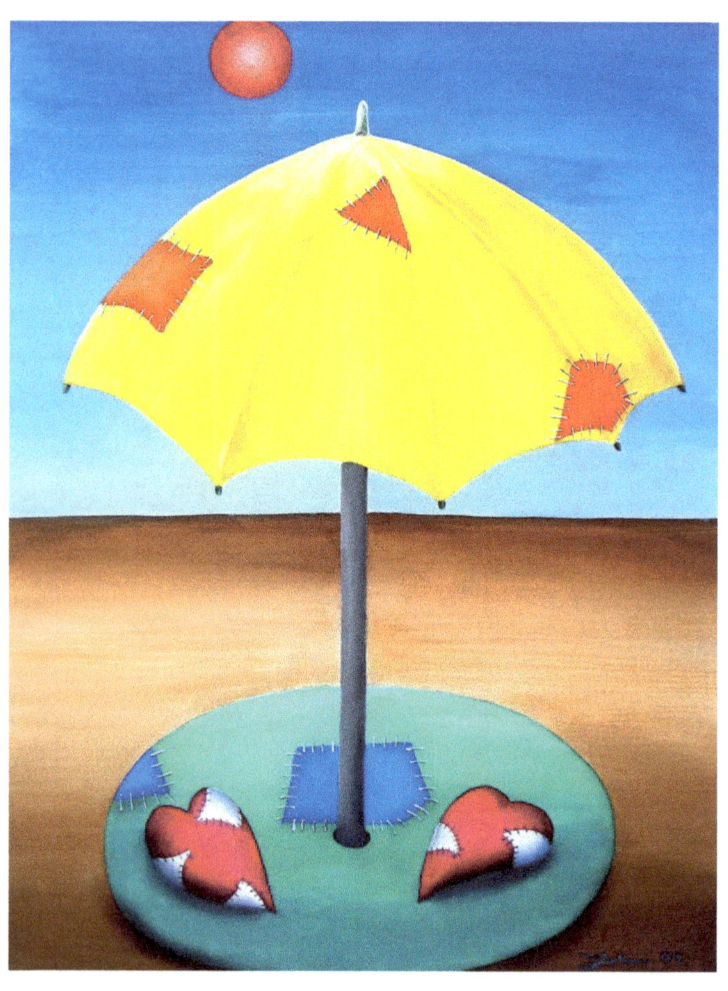

破碎的心依然相信爱情 / A Broken Heart Still Believes in Love

丙烯画 / Acrylic Painting。 78X100 CM. 2000.

82

悼论是你缴了多年的房租

却没能把年龄留下来过夜

A paradox is paying rent for years

Yet you can't persuade your age to stay the night

83

很多故事讲完后才有发生的理由

Many stories have a reason to take place only after they are told

84

很多人至今不明白

成年人是终生职业

Many people still don't understand to this day

Being an adult is a lifelong career

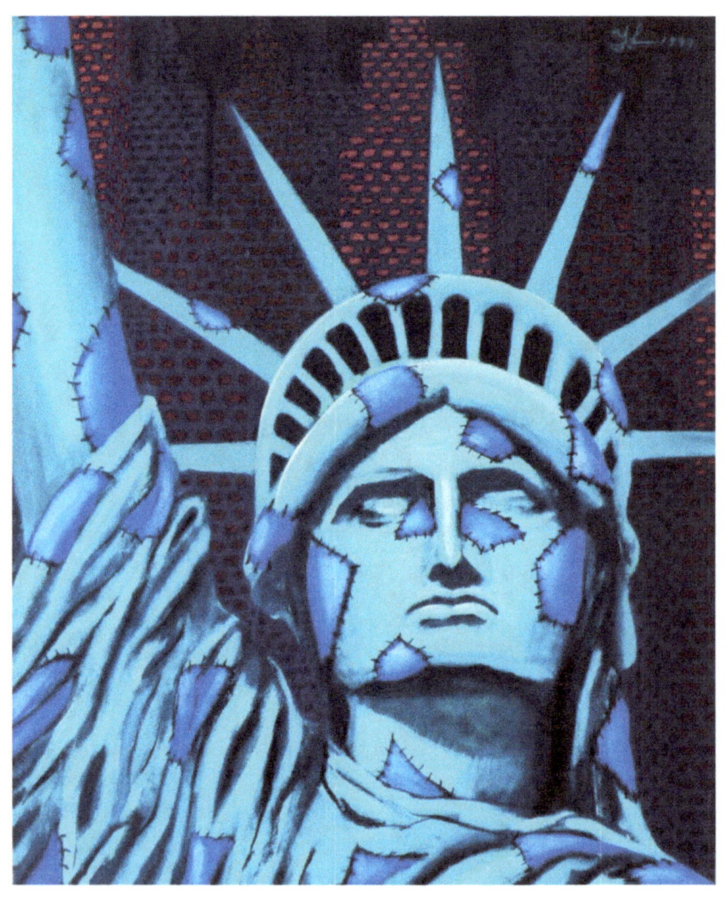

自由更需要修补 / Freedom Needs Mending Even More

丙烯画 / Acrylic Painting。 78X100 CM. 1999.

85

黑胶唱片喜欢摩擦寿命的旋转

Vinyl records enjoy the spinning that wears down lifespan

86

虚荣使进化打了折扣

Vanity compromises evolution

冲动形成了草率的线条

那不是练习出来的笔法

Impulsiveness results in sloppy lines

That is not brushwork honed through practice

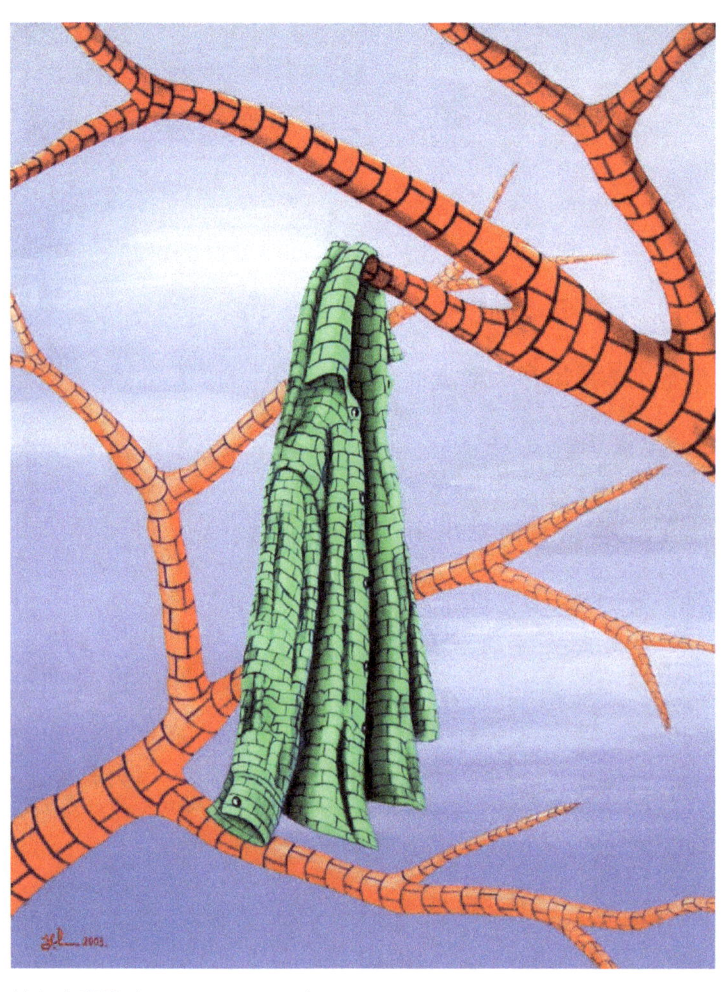

挂在寂寞里 / Hanging in Loneliness

丙烯画 / Acrylic Painting。 76X100 CM. 2003.

88

在古董市场上我捡漏了

陶罐上的半截闪电

出售者告诉我那是裂纹

I found a bargain at the antique market

Half a bolt of lightning was on a ceramic jar

The seller told me it was only a crack

89

龙在文化里横行千年

没担心过灭绝的危险

Dragons have run amok in culture for thousands of years

Without fearing extinction

垄断与专利是同父异母的兄弟

Monopolies and patents are brothers born of the same father but different mothers

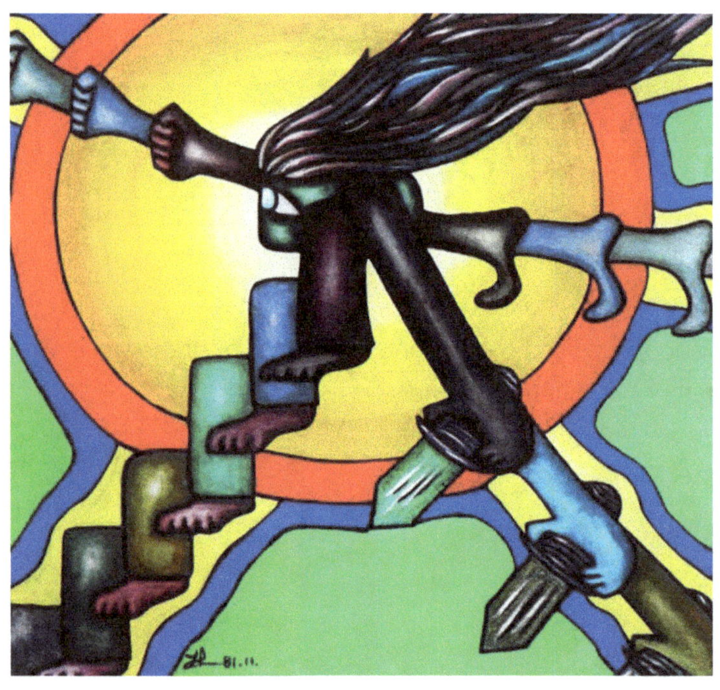

仇恨的力度 / The Force of Hatred

油画 / Oil Painting。 70X72 CM. 1981.

91

拳头不算什么

被双乳击倒的人更多

A fist is no big deal

More people have been knocked over by a pair of breasts

92

在工业革命之前

草药是直接长出来的化学

Before the industrial revolution

Herbal medicine was chemistry grown directly from the earth

你的成就必须蘸点醋

才能让百姓想起饺子

Your achievements must be dipped in vinegar

Only then will people think about dumplings

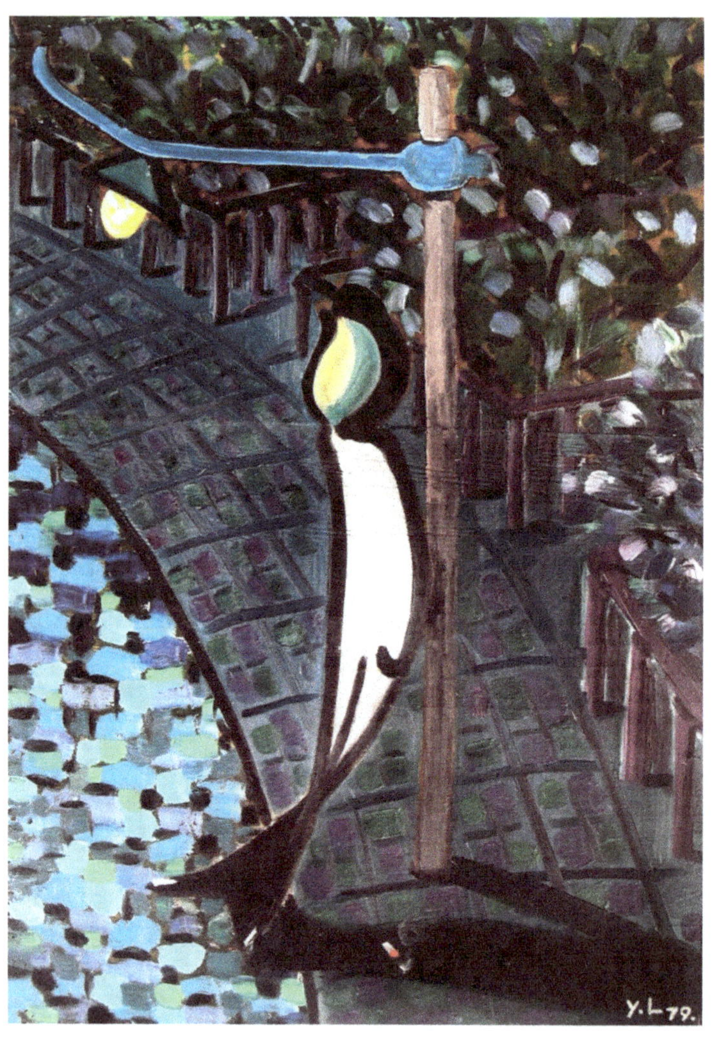

游荡 / Wandering

油画 / Oil Painting。 44X58 CM. 1979.

94

国家的尺寸都是战争测量出来的

A country's size is always measured by war

95

解决了自然里的豺狼虎豹

就由人类扮演各种动物了

Having dealt with nature's jackals, wolves, tigers and
leopards

Humans now play the roles of each kind of animal

96

人间到处都有

逼迫青蛙脱掉迷彩服

改穿食品包装的现象

A phenomenon exists among people everywhere

They force frogs to take off their camouflage attire

And change into food packaging

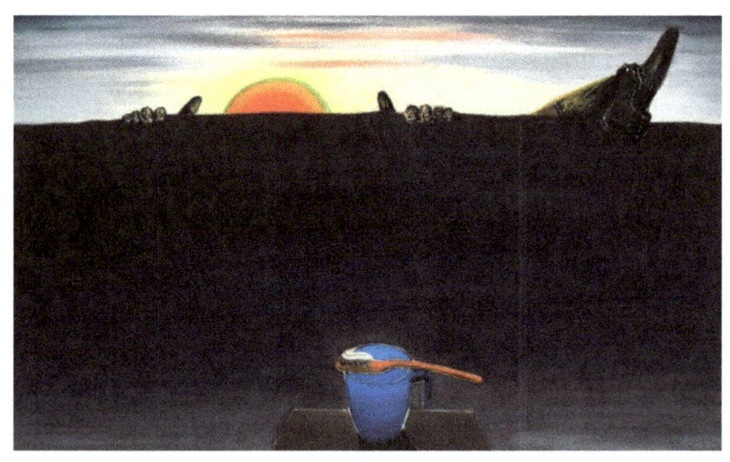

从地平线上爬上来刷牙的太阳

The Sun Crawling Up from the Horizon to Brush Its Teeth

油画 / Oil Painting。 60X120 CM. 1981.

97

人生的最佳忠告出炉了：

别为那款好药去生一场病

The best advice for life is fresh out of the oven

Don't get sick for the sake of good medicine

98

一个茶商对我说

情绪不稳的时候

茶香是有扶手的

A tea purveyor told me

When emotions are unsettled

The fragrance of tea has armrests

99

花朵以自身的速度凋谢

不会保持某个姿势等你拍照

Flowers wither at their own pace

They won't hold a pose for you to take a picture

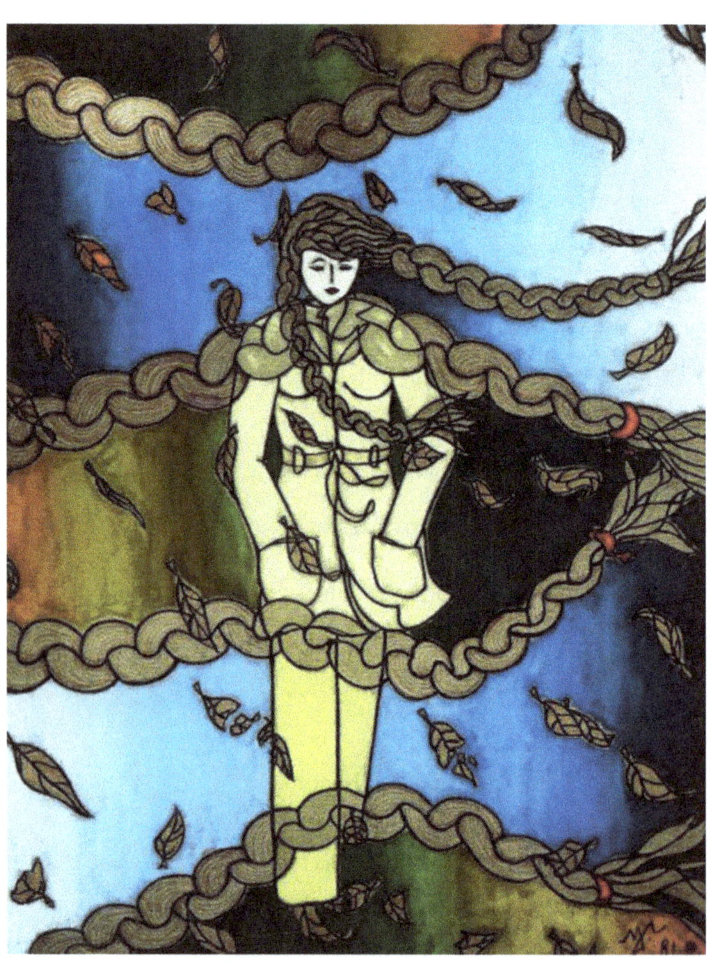

秋恋 / Autumn Love

油画 / Oil Painting。 86X120 CM. 1981.

100

在恶性的社会事件里

我看到了被拐骗的正午几年后回来了

手上还牵着一个无辜的黄昏

In an ugly social incident

I saw the abducted noon come back after several years

Leading the innocent dusk by its hands

101

文学战壕的说法

是指你蹲在那儿抽烟时的

经典造型

The term literary trenches

Refers to that classic pose

Of you just squatting there smoking a cigarette

枪的长相和造型

也是丰富甚至美观的

类似众人各异的面貌

最好别配备脏话和子弹

The looks and models of guns

Are varied and beautiful

Like the many different faces of people

Best not to arm them with profanity and bullets

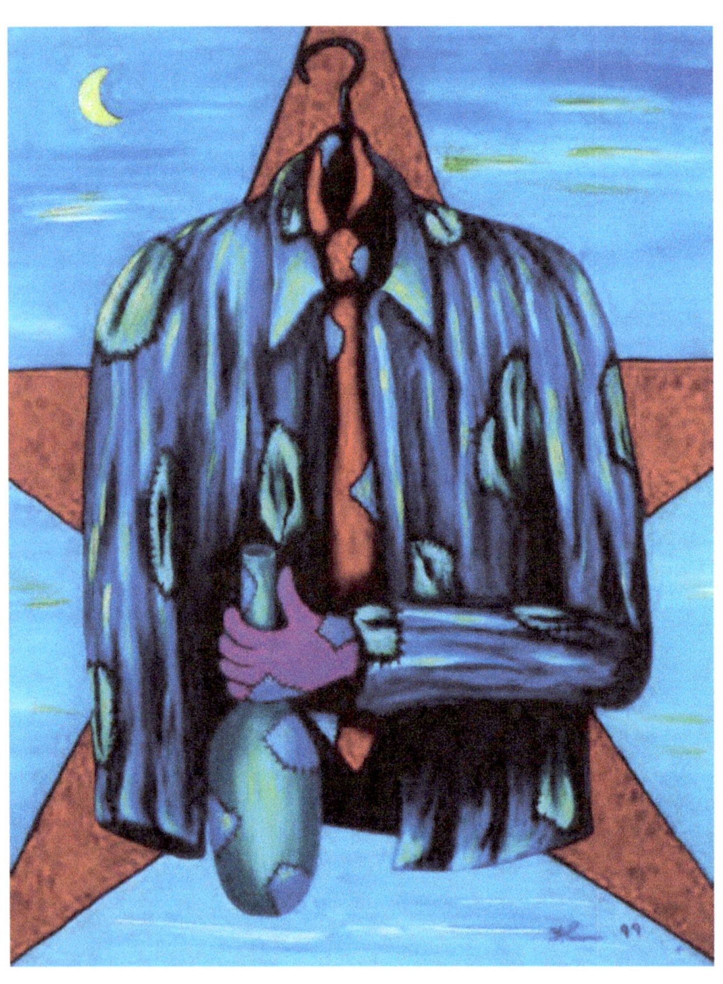

诗人风度 / A Poet's Bearing

丙烯画 / Acrylic Painting。 76X100 CM. 1999.

文不文明的现象

是形而上下拉扯出来的

妥协的线条是常见的流行

The phenomena of civility and incivility

Are pulled between the metaphysical and material worlds

The trend we often see is lines of compromise

104

捂着心窝感受心曲的播放

至于刻进了掌心的是什么

只有本人知道

With your hand over heart feel its song play

As for what's engraved in your palm

Only you know

105

窗外开阔的景色

也是坐电梯上来的

The expansive scenery outside the window

Also came up by the elevator

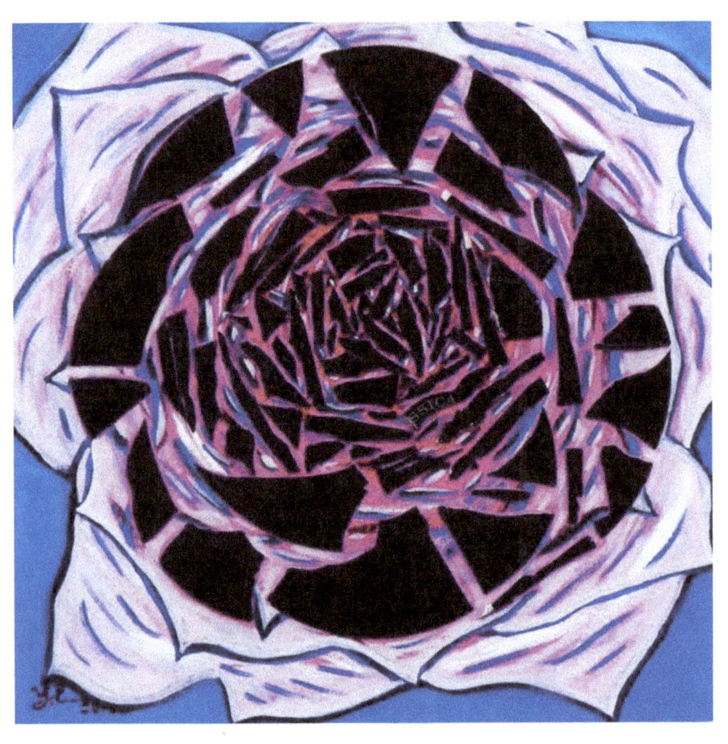

开放成玫瑰的唱片 / A Record Opening into a Rose
丙烯、黑胶唱片 / Acrylic, Vinyl Record。 62X62 CM. 2010.

106

创作过程是时间的内循环

它因消化我大脑的分泌物

而上瘾

The creative process is time's internal cycle

Because it consumes my brain's secretions

It addicts

107

单翅飞翔的鸟

有其独特的天地

唯艺术喜欢这样的神来之笔

A bird flying with one wing

Has its unique world

Only art loves such a divine stroke

众人的口水为事件的名声解渴

The crowd's saliva satisfies the thirst for how incidents are
regarded

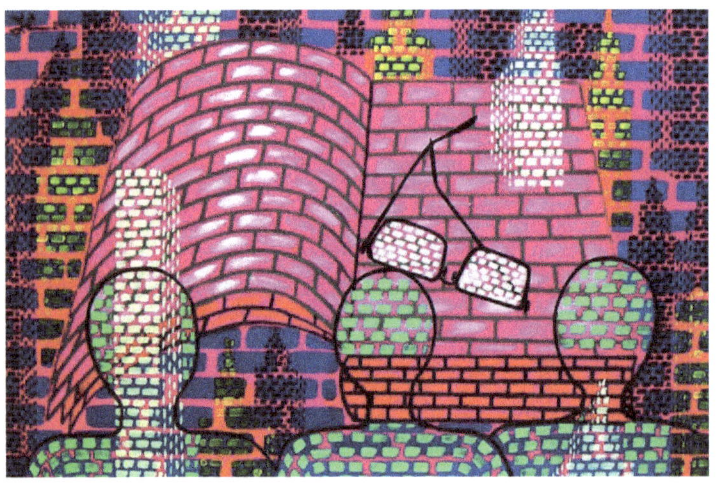

阅读 / Reading

丙烯画 / Acrylic Painting。 70X110 CM. 2007.

高度数的政治

为了制造时代的酒鬼

High-proof politics

Exists to manufacture an era's drunkards

110

世俗是一面没有想象力的镜子

就像大自然

从不参考人类生活的提纲

The everyday world is a mirror without imagination

As with Nature

It never refers back to the template of human life

111

在无风的日子里

姓风的依然姓风

On days without Wind

Wind still bears the name Wind

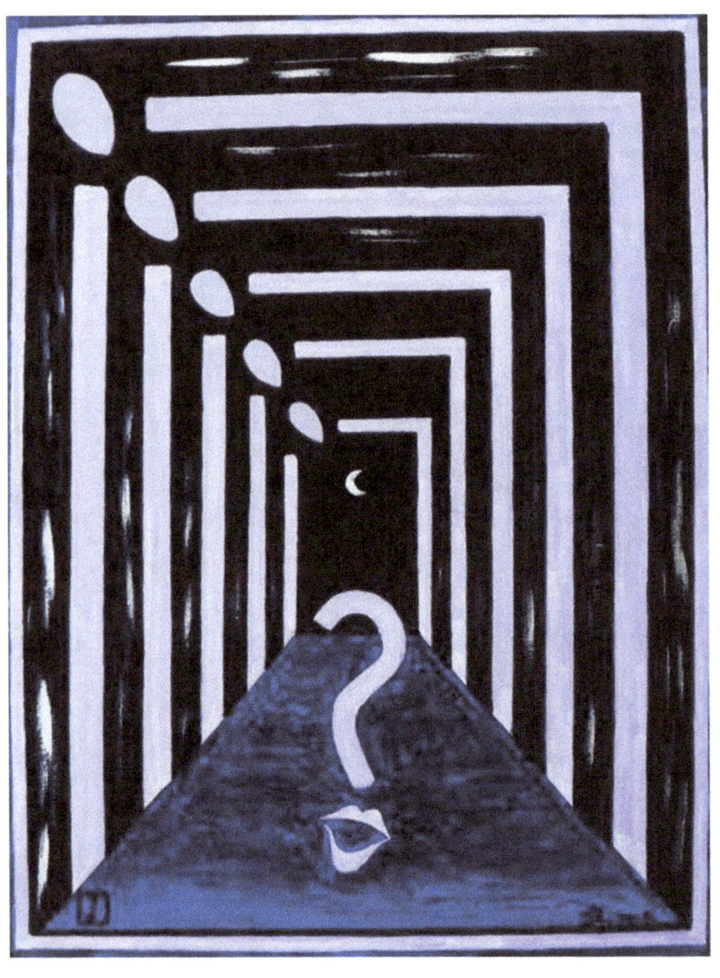

门的联想 / Associations of a Door

木板、喷漆 / Wooden Board, Spray Paint。 44X58 CM. 1979.

没有翅膀就已降落祖国

AI 找不到我出生的原图

也不知道憋足一辈子的气

等于入水多少年

Having landed in my motherland without wings

AI can't find the blueprint of my birth

Nor does it know how many years submerged underwater

Equals a lifetime of holding my breath

113

人都有离开社会之后

却又回不了家的尴尬

After leaving society

Everyone knows the awkwardness of being unable to go home

这几年寻人启事不少

很多敏感词都离家出走了

There are more missing person notices these days

Many sensitive words have run away from home

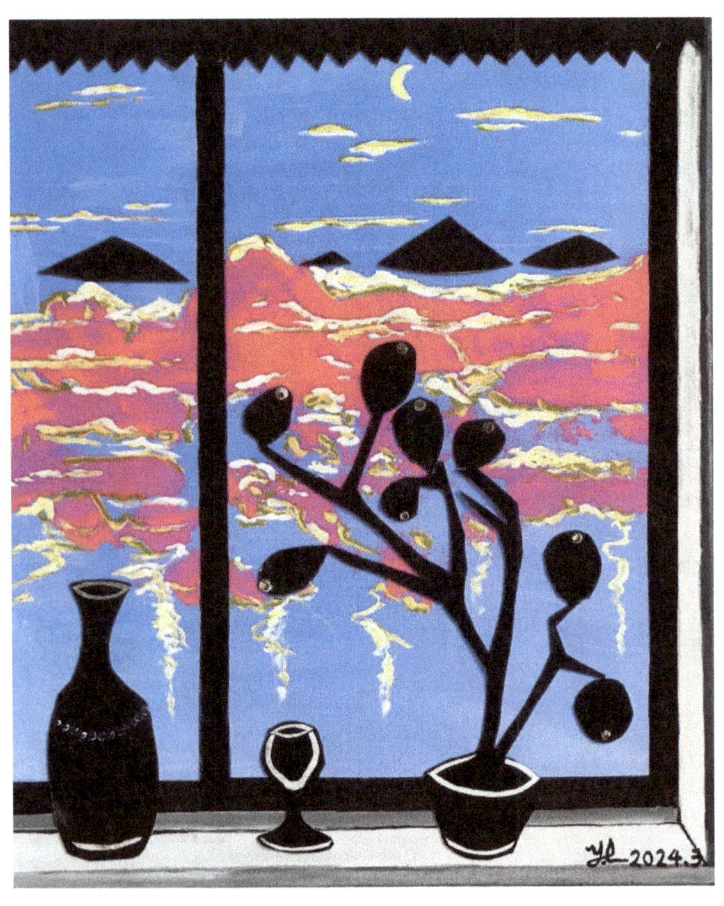

窗外 / Outside the Window

丙烯画 / Acrylic Painting。 40X56 CM. 2024.

115

圆能把杯子上的嘴喝出残缺

Roundness drinks a flaw into the mouth on a cup

116

有谁能代表雨来谈谈

上天入地的

不同感受吗

Who can speak

For rain's different sensations

Ascending to the heavens or entering the earth

117

工业社会货架上的大众

都具有备用螺丝的幸福

People on industrial society's shelves

Share the happiness of being spare screws

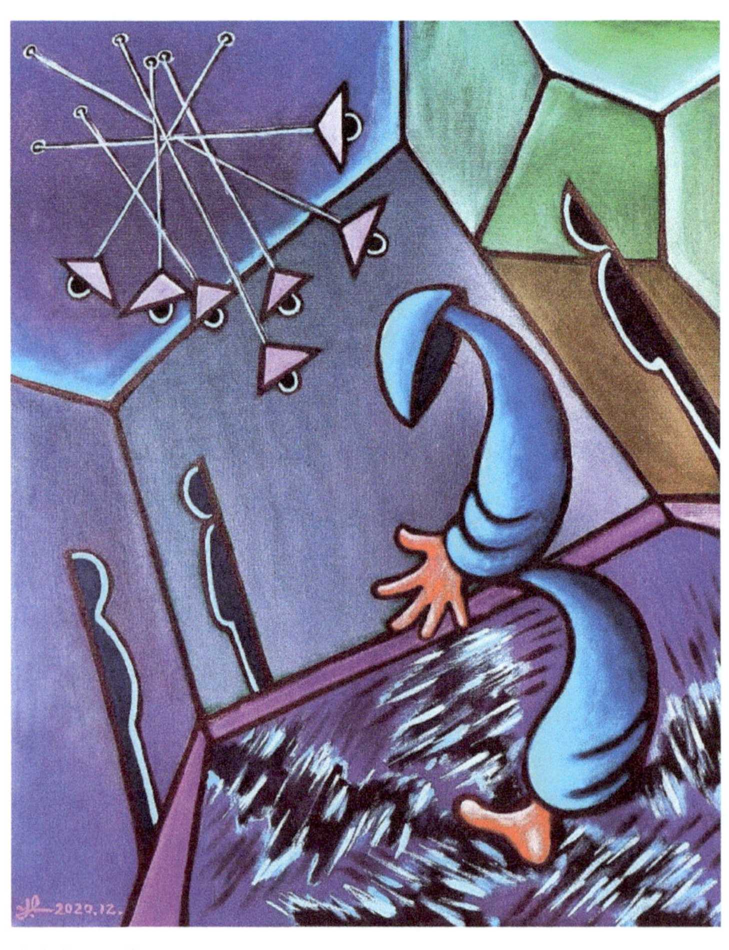

室内的个人危机 / An Indoor Personal Crisis

丙烯画 / Acrylic Painting。 60X76 CM. 2020.

118

在很多本国家字典里

沉默的定义也具有说的意思

In many of our country's dictionaries

Silence's definition also includes speaking

119

方向性的红漆又刷了一遍方向

Directional red paint has painted over its direction again

120

当代数学

以大楼的层高丈量窗户里的人

In contemporary mathematics

People in windows are measured by the heights of their buildings

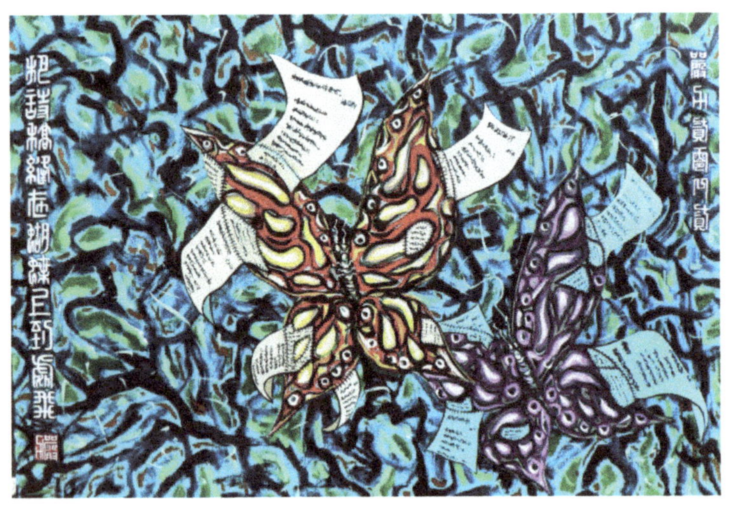

把诗稿缝在蝴蝶上到处飞

Sewing a Poem Manuscript onto a Butterfly to Fly Everywhere

丙烯画 / Acrylic Painting。 60X158 CM. 2012.

121

我们都希望在 23 世纪之前

轰炸机能成为养在笼子里的宠物

We all hope that by the 23rd century

Bomber planes can become pets raised in a cage

122

持久的意志力一如指甲

以内在的火力稳步向前

Sustained willpower is like a fingernail

Advancing steadily with an inner force

123

装睡是受昏暗岁月的催眠

可惜温床睡不醒自我

Feigned sleep is the hypnosis of dark times

A hotbed sadly does not waken the self

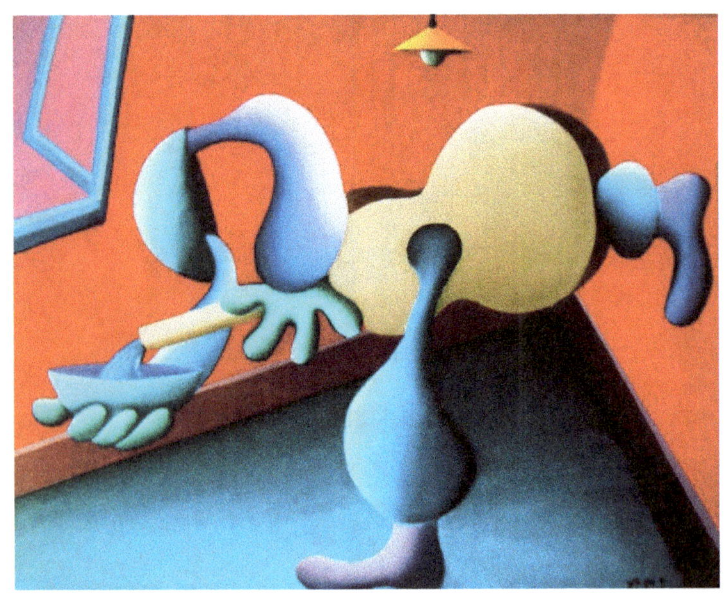

喝音乐 / Drinking Music

油画 / Oil Painting。 76X100 CM. 1984.

事实证明神在人间碰壁成了教堂

Facts prove that God became a church after hitting the wall in the human world

125

风没有阴、阳

力量不分雌、雄

对它们的描述

则有着男、女之分

Wind has no yin or yang

And strength is not feminine or masculine

Only the descriptions of them

Are divided into male and female

126

我垂钓游动着思想的波浪

I fish waves for swimming thoughts

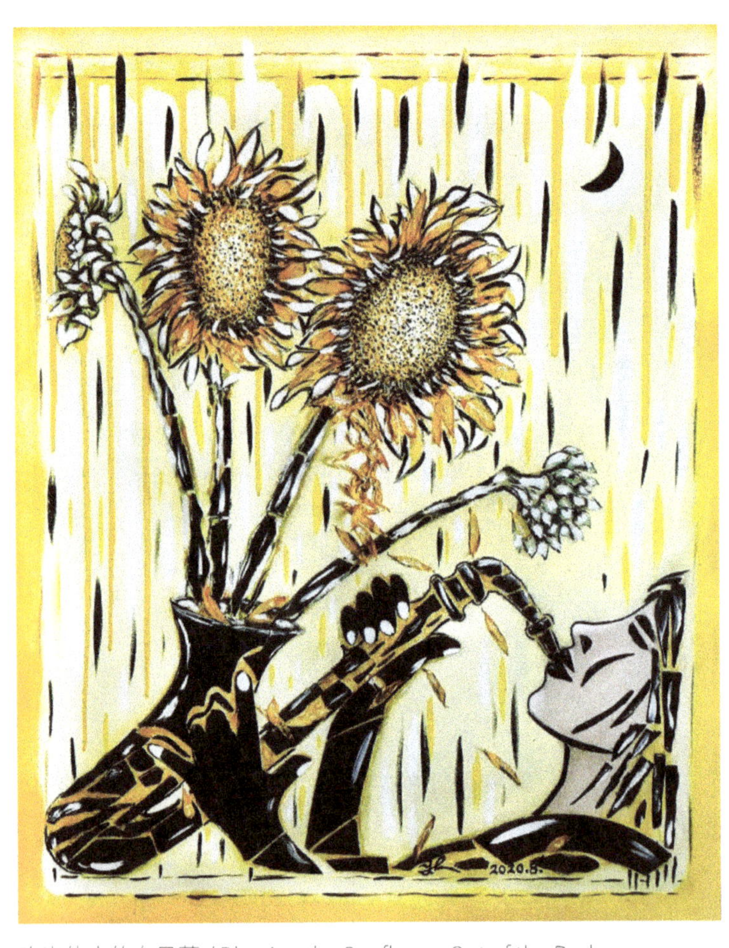

吹出体内的向日葵 / Blowing the Sunflower Out of the Body

丙烯画 / Acrylic Painting。 60X76 CM. 2020.

127

苍蝇和蚊子是你每天遇到最多的熟人

Flies and mosquitoes are the familiar people you bump into
most often each day

128

见鬼就是在没有鬼的地方

见到了扮鬼的人

Seeing ghosts where there are none is simply

Seeing people acting as ghosts

129

目光所及处

有很多段历史没有背影

As far as the eye can see

Many periods of history left no backshadow

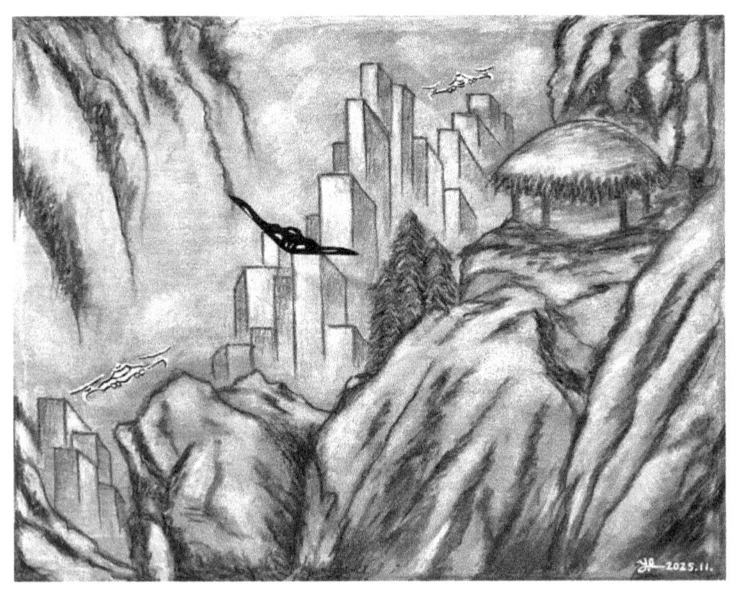

与大自然共存的时代 / An Era of Coexistence with Nature

丙烯画 / Acrylic Painting。60X76 CM. 2020.

130

饿成一把刀的人

一生都在切面包

People starved into becoming knives

Spend their lives cutting bread

严力（诗人、艺术家）1954 年生于北京。1973 年开始诗歌创作，1979 年开始绘画创作。是 1979 年北京先锋艺术团体"星星画会"和文学团体"今天"的成员。参加的第一次集体展是 1979 年的星星画展，1984 年在上海人民公园展览厅举办了国内最早的先锋艺术的个人画展。1985 年从北京留学美国并于 1987 年在纽约创立"一行"诗刊（2000 年停刊），2019 年 6 月《一行》杂志在纽约复刊。继续任主编。2018 年出任纽约"法拉盛诗歌节"主任委员，同年出任纽约"海外华文作家笔会"会长。

Yan Li (poet and Artist. b. 1954, Beijing, China) is a member of a group of artists known as The Stars; as a poet, he is identified with the Misty Poets; His first art exhibited at 1979. And He exhibited first one man show in 1984 at people's park in Shanghai China, This is also the first one-man Avant garde art show after 1949 in China.

In 1987, he founded First Line in New York; the publication is a quarterly journal that features the works of contemporary Chinese poets as well as translations of American poems. and was editor in chief (ceased publication in 2000) and reissued in June 2020 as semi-annual magazine. He became chairman of the Flushing Poetry Festival in New York from 2018. And the chairman of the Overseas Chinese Writers'Pen Association in New York.

斯仲达 毕业于康州大学，主修汉语，1982 年前往北京大学进一步深造。居住北京期间，他认识了严力及阮丹青，至今与他们保持深厚的友谊。在《一行》诗人社团由严力创办时，斯仲达是成员之一，他的中文诗歌刊登于《一行》创刊最初几期。自 1982 年起，他便深入参与与中国有关的商业活动，并持续数十年。1992 年至 2020 年间，他长居香港，创立并经营专注于中国市场的顾问公司——斯马国有限公司。多年来，他始终与中国文化，艺术及诗歌保持紧密联系。

Glen Steinman majored in Chinese language studies at Connecticut College and continued his studies at Beijing University in 1982. While in Beijing, he met Yan Li and Danching Ruan. His close friendships with them continue today. He was a member of First Line upon its founding by Yan Li, and his Chinese-language poems were published in the first issues of First Line magazine. His deep, decades-long involvement in China-related business began in 1982. From 1992-2020, he lived in Hong Kong where he founded and operated Seema International Limited, a China-focused advisory firm. Throughout the years, he has maintained a close connection to Chinese culture, art and poetry.

阮丹青 是香港浸会大学社会学荣休教授。她本科毕业于北京大学西语系；1993 获得美国哥伦比亚大学社会学博士学位。她的主要研究领域包括社会网络，特别是东西方人际关系模式的比较和社会阶层与流动。论文发表于社会网络（美国），国际移民研究学刊（美国），社会学（法国），中国研究（澳大利亚），中国社会科学（中国），社会学研究(中国)等学术刊物。她也从事了关于中国改革开放初期工业改革的口述史研究（合作者：定宜庄 杨善华，相关著作由牛津大学出版社和三联出版社出版）。她目前的研究课题是关于精英的再生产。她在上世纪 80 年代认识了斯仲達和严力，成为了好朋友。

Danching Ruan is Professor Emeritus of Sociology at Hong Kong Baptist University. She received her BA degree from Peking University and her PhD degree from Columbia University. Her main research interests are in the fields of social network analysis, social stratification, and social inequality. She has also worked on historical case studies of the early period of China's economic reform and has published with Oxford University Press and Joint Publishing. Her writings have also been published in Social Forces, Social Networks, The China Journal, International Migration Review, American Behavioral Scientist, Social Sciences in China, L'Année Sociologique, among others. Her current research focuses on the issue of elite reproduction: cultural and social capital reproduction in urban China under Mao. Her good friendships with Glen Steinman and Yan Li began in the early 1980's.